THE BUN FESTIVAL OF CHEUNG CHAU

長 洲 太 平 清 醮

THE BUN FESTIVAL OF CHEUNG CHAU

長 洲 太 平 清 醮

Introduction: Jonathan Chamberlain
Photographs: Ian Lambot

Studio Publications

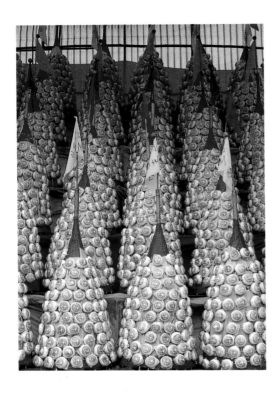

Design: Ian Lambot and Helen Smith
Translation and production: Emmy Lung

All photographs © 1983 1986 Ian Lambot
The Bun Festival © 1990 Jonathan
   Chamberlain
Copyright © 1990 Studio Publications

Colour Separation by Evergreen Colour
   Separation (Scanning) Co. Ltd
Printed by Everbest Printing Company Ltd

ISBN 962 7460 03 6

太 平 清 醮

The Bun Festival

長洲四面環海,兩頭山崗,中央狹長,地形如
啞鈴,且位於香港西南十一里,剛好被大嶼山
環抱。長洲面積雖然少於一平方公里,却是香港
人口最多的離島——現今約有居民五至六萬。
其實,早在五千年前,長洲已有人居住,而發展至
現在,島上更居住了鶴佬、潮州、客家、蛋家及
土生廣東人。

　　這小島與海盜似有淵源——中國著名海盜
張保仔曾在此處南端的山洞避難。可是,長洲
是海盜避難所這傳說,却並不十分可信。事實上,
自一八四〇年至一八九八年——即決定性的
"九十九年"條約簽訂以前,長洲主要是一個中
國關口,負責徵收進出香港的貿易稅項。

　　長洲的北帝廟——即玉虛宮,正好面向西南
往來澳門的水翼船通道,而石鼓洲就好像是
庇護屏障,防止污穢流入廟內。每逢農曆四月,
北帝廟前的康樂廣場,更會舉行 "玄天上帝太平
清醮",或稱 "打醮"——即超渡水陸游魂,而
外國人則喜歡稱之為 "包山節"。

　　稱為 "包山節",原因是每逢醮期,三座由竹
架起、高五十呎、堆滿幽包的大包山都會在
北帝廟前的康樂廣場出現。不可缺少的當然還有
每邊三十六座的小包山。包山前面、廣場的中央,
是一座以竹和蓆所搭成的大戲棚。那裏,一場接

Cheung Chau is a small island made up of
two rocky headlands connected by a sand
spit, giving it a distinctive barbell shape.
It lies 11 miles south-west of Hong Kong,
cradled within the embrace of the far larger
neighbouring island of Lantau. Despite being
less than one square mile in area, its popu-
lation, the largest of all Hong Kong's out-
lying islands, is now estimated at more than
50,000. The island has been continuosly
inhabited for some 5000 years. Its current
residents include many different communities of Chinese people: the Hoklo, Chui
Chow and Hakka, the fishing people known
as Tanka, as well as the local Cantonese.

　　The island also boasts a slim connec-
tion with piracy: the great Chinese pirate,
Cheung Po Chai, is once supposed to have
hidden in a cave at the southern tip of the
island. But the belief that Cheung Chau was
a pirates' haven is unsupported. From the
1840s till 1898, when the fateful 99-year
treaty between Britain and China was
signed, Cheung Chau was a Chinese customs post, levying charges on all traffic
passing in and out of Hong Kong.

　　The Pak Tai temple on Cheung Chau
(or, to give it its correct name, 'The Palace of
the Jade Void') faces south-west down the
channel where scurrying hydrofoils head for
Macau. The small island of Shek Kwu Chau,
out in the channel, acts as a 'spirit screen',
protecting the temple entrance from any
invasion of pestilential spirits. Here, in the
forecourt of the temple, during the first half
of the fourth month of the Chinese calendar,
the *Yuen Tin Seung Tai Tai-Ping Ching Chui*
takes place. Literally the name means the
"Clear (ie vegetarian) Festival for Praying for
Safety, overseen by the Superior Ruler of the
Dark Heavens". It is also referred to as a *Ta
Chiu*, a festival for dispelling troublesome

spirits, or 'hungry ghosts'. In English, the festival is better known as the Cheung Chau Bun Festival.

This is because of the three tall 'bun mountains', which are erected for the festival on the opposite side of the forecourt facing the temple. Built of bamboo to a height of more than 50 feet, these are wrapped with strings of fluffy white steamed buns. On either side, on shelves, are 36 smaller cones of buns. In front of the bun towers, in the centre of the courtyard, a huge, open bamboo and mat-shed opera house is built, where, for the three days and nights of the festival, an opera troupe performs historical plays. The orchestra, sitting in the wings, accompanies the high-pitched singers with the wailing, percussive music appropriate to this art form. Between this building and the towers is another temporary stall in which three large, fiery-visaged papier-maché figures survey the scene. They are surrounded by a cluster of smaller grey-cloaked figures and, in front of them, an oil drum accepts the burning offerings that are made continuously throughout the festival.

Up the steps, at the level of the temple itself, there are two further stalls. In one, three Taoist priests dance or chant for the duration of the festivities. Their stall is hung with scriptures painted on to silk banners. In the other stall, the most-venerated black statue of Pak Tai, Emperor of the North and Ruler of the Dark Heavens, plays host to serried ranks of god statues brought in homage from all the other temples and shrines on the island, especially those of the street and neighbourhood associations around which the political and cultural life of the town is focussed. They are brought, on the first day of the festival, in great pomp

一場的神功戲三日三夜不停地上演。坐在兩旁的樂師，演奏着低沉的絃樂、高亢的敲擊樂，配合着演員高音調的演繹，在在表現出這種中國傳統戲劇的特色。在廟宇與包山之間，供奉着三個由混凝紙造成的神像，威風凜凜的省覽整個醮場。而圍繞着祂們的，就是一羣體積較小的灰色神像，神像面前更放着一個焚化爐，供善信燃燒祭品，香火十分鼎盛。

拾級而上，位於廟宇旁的是大法師棚和神壇。大法師就在掛滿一幅一幅經文的棚中，為大典唸經禱告。神壇中，則供奉着最受崇敬的黑色北帝像。祂就在那裏，迎接各廟宇殿堂諸神來朝──尤其是那些位於長洲大街小巷的政治文化重點及社團組織的諸神。就在迎神日那天，打扮得一身莊嚴華麗的諸神，在鼓鑼喧天的樂聲中，像守護神一樣，駕臨建醮場地。

除此以外，長洲各社團組織的醒獅麒麟都紛紛到場，等待點睛。每當兩隊獅隊途中相遇，他們必會擺姿弄勢，以期互相示威一番。然後，獅隊便會四出為各家各戶祈福，而人們亦會興高彩烈的掛起利是來迎接他們。有些人更把利是掛得高高，以期考驗精力充沛的醒獅隊員。

鶴佬是長洲很有影響力的一羣,透過他們特別
有一隻角的麒麟,我們也可猜到一二。另外,依照
鶴佬傳統,有一隻大角的麒麟是向天起舞的,
而有一隻小角的則是在地上滾出不同舞姿。

醮場的兩邊,更有很多小販售買價廉而
炫麗的風車和塑膠造的驅魔劍。這嘻嘻哈哈的
場面,都為會場帶來不少歡樂的氣氛。但到底,
最吸引的還是"包山節"本身。

至今,"包山節"一項仍然令人嘆為觀止的
項目,就是會景巡遊中的飄色。每一隊飄色隊
都有兩位小孩子,由特別設計的支架撐起,
並打扮成傳說中的主角或是歷史人物。這邊廂,
小男孩站立在小女孩手中左搖右擺的扇子上;
那邊廂,小女孩被發現在煙的一端嘗試平衡。
如此花心思建成的飄色,相信是發展自兩次大戰
期間,因為關於這世紀初的會景巡遊,當時的記
記載仍未有提及現今這巧妙的設計:"每一條村
都派出隊伍參加飄色,競爭十分激烈。帶頭的
是一條龍……隨後的人托着一個平台,平台
上面,是兩個塗了脂粉、穿着華麗服裝的女孩。"

發展至今,每一座飄色設計都有一男一女,
被挑選參加的,年齡約在五至九歲之間,身高
約四十二吋。事實上,要站立在色櫃上維持固定

by gaily dressed 'guards of honour' accompanied by the clash of cymbals, reedy wailings of flutes and the numbing rhythms of drums.

With them also come the lion-dance troupes of each association, seeking blessings for their 'lions'. Should two lions meet there will be a mock battle involving much posturing and strutting. Later, each lion-dance team will tour its own patch, dancing at each premises where it is welcomed by a gift of *laisee*, the ubiquitous red packet containing 'lucky money'. This is usually placed in a tricky position to test the mettle of the lion dancers. A strong Hoklo influence can be seen in the presence of lions with a distinctive horn. According to Hoklo tradition, those with a large horn wave their heads high in the air, and those with a small horn wave their heads close to the ground.

On the fringes of the scene stand sellers of gaudy whirligigs and plastic exorcism swords. It all adds up to a bustling hurly-burly of excitement. But there is more to the Bun Festival than just all this activity.

The main feature of the festival as it is known today is the procession of floats around the town. Each float consists of two children set up in a cunningly contrived tableau portraying some message or other of a topical or historical nature. Here a boy will appear to be standing on the fluttering fan held in a girl's hand, there a girl will balance unconcernedly on the end of a cigarette. It appears, however, that these sophisticated floats may be a development dating from between the wars. A description of the parade dating from early this century makes no mention of the clever devices now used: "Each village street provides a procession, and there is a great emulation between teams. At its head is a dragon ... (which is) followed by bearers carrying a platform covered with a canopy, and on the platform two girls, powdered and painted to the eyes and clad in gay garments."

Nowadays, each float usually consists of a boy and girl pair, aged between five and nine and standing around 42 inches tall. It is a gruelling task for them as they have to stand still and remain relatively good-natured for up to three or four hours at a time. It has sometimes been rumoured that they are drugged; how else can they cope with the ordeal so well? In fact, people involved laugh at the suggestion and it must be admitted that drugging a child is likely to be counter-productive; they need to keep their wits about them. For the children, it is a great honour to be chosen and it is enough that they are tremendously awed by their responsibilities. This explains their solemn, sometimes slightly dazed expression.

The child at the bottom of the tableau has an easier time than the one suspended precariously in the air. The contrivance is managed by running a carefully shaped iron rod up the side of the lower child and along his arm, then up through a decorative item to a metal footrest concealed in one of the upper child's shoes. The rod then continues up inside the clothing of the upper child, with a semi-circular hoop at the top encir-cling his or her back. Half-way up there is a small seat to sit on, from which a second support extends down. The children are securely strapped into place and great care is taken to keep them comfortable.

Umbrellas are at hand to shade them from the sun or rain and, when the parade stops, long forked sticks are raised so that the children can rest against them. The children are certainly more comfortable than the men and women (mainly women) whose job it is to carry the tableaux on their shoulders using bamboo poles and

姿勢三至四小時之久，是一件使人非常筋疲力倦的差使。有些傳聞，更猜測小孩子所以能支持那麼久，是因為吃了藥物──似乎沒有別的原因解釋他們超乎常人的耐力？可是，負責人却回應笑道：若果眞有其事，反而會有反效果，因為他們又要另想辦法使小孩子清醒理智。眞正原因是被選中的小孩，會以為被委以重任，因而感到十分光榮，所以他們會特別隆重其事，時時打醒十二分精神。這或可解釋他們嚴肅，甚至有點茫然的神情。

有時候，在下面的小孩要比在色櫃上的舒服一點。這飄色的設計，是利用一條鐵竿，沿着下面小孩的手臂伸展出來，連接上面小孩的腳座。然後鐵竿一直再沿着上面小孩的身體再伸展，直至一個半圓鐵環圍繞着背部。約在身體一半的位置，更有一張小小的椅，供小孩歇息時坐；而另一條鐵竿，就自椅子向下伸展，支持小孩的另一條腿。於是，小孩就穩固地確定了位置，亦保障自然舒服。另外，小孩手中的傘子可供他阻擋日晒雨淋；每逢巡遊隊伍停下來，就有一支叉狀支架給小孩依傍。當然，在

色櫃上的小孩還是比成人（主要女性）舒服，
因為後者的工作是用竹竿和繩索把色櫃抬在
肩膊。可是，現在有些色櫃是放在手推車上的，
這樣小孩便沒有那麼舒服了。

　　飄色是長洲太平清醮的特色之一，沒有別的
地方可以媲美。飄色相傳源自廣東省的潮州
和福建省，可是沒有人能確實它真正的起源。
另外，亦有相傳佛山是其發源地。而有關一八
四〇年星加坡天后誕的記載是這樣的：
「……特別吸引觀眾的是飄色中的主角：只有
五至六歲的小女孩，身穿特別奪目耀眼的
中國傳統服裝，被藏在衣服裏的鐵竿支撐着……
另外更有傘子替她們遮風擋雨。」由於很多
星加坡華人都來自潮州和福建，所以很可能
兩地的飄色均源自同一地方。歌倫·拍克在其
所著的《中國信條與習俗》一書中，亦曾經提及
中國江蘇省的飄色：「小女孩站在用木做的
平台上，用長竿支撐着，由男人抬着……和
……這飄色就是為了驅走孤魂野鬼。」

　　似乎，驅走孤魂野鬼都是三個節日的共同
目標。他們似乎要透過展示自己的女兒，以搏取
神的同情。這樣看來，這些女孩子豈非成了
奴役的貢品？這又是否暗示正因他們只有女兒，

ropes. Some of the tableaux are now pushed around on trolleys, but these are not so comfortable for the children.

The procession of tableaux is a feature of the festival that has few parallels. It is supposed to have originated from somewhere in the Chiu Chow districts on the border of Guangdong and Fujian provinces but no-one seems to know the exact location of this original inspiration: the town of Foshan has been suggested as one source. Interestingly, a description of a festival in honour of Tin Hau, goddess of fishermen, that first took place in Singapore as long ago as 1840 says: "... what particularly engaged the attention of the spectators, and was the chief feature of the procession, were the little girls from five to eight years of age carried aloft in groups on gaily ornamented platforms dressed in every variety of Tartar and Chinese costumes. The little creatures were supported in their place by iron rods, which were concealed under their clothes ... every care being taken to shield them with umbrellas." Since many of the Singaporean Chinese hail from the Chiu Chow areas of Fujian province, it is obvious that these festivals share the same origin. Colonel Burkhardt, author of *Chinese Creeds and Customs*, mentions another source in Gansu Province in the north of China where, "small girls standing on a wooden platform, surmounting a long pole, were carried by men ... and ... (this) procession (was) mounted to ward off pestilence."

Warding off pestilence is certainly the aim that unites all these three festivals. It appears that people seek to earn heaven's pity by showing off their female children. Are the girls a form of slave tribute? Are they a sign that the people only have girls, not boys, and so have suffered enough from pestilence? Are the adults asking the heavens to take pity on the children? The symbolism, or underlying meaning, needs teasing out.

The Bun Festival, then, is a cleansing festival, but while such festivals may be common they do not usually occur so frequently or on such a scale. On Cheung Chau the festival is held every year; elsewhere they may be conducted only once every decade. Cleansing is required to combat 'pollution' and, for the Chinese, pollution is brought about by bad spirits, often identified with the 'hungry ghosts'. On Cheung Chau, the pollution is clearly held to be more severe than other places. Why should this be so?

The answer may be found in the island's main cemetery, where there is a large communal grave-mound dedicated to the souls of the unnamed dead. This is a feature of many Chinese cemeteries. Wealthy men gain credit by building a grave for the remains of those who die without families to care for them, or who have died far from home or in times of war. Such dead, being uncared for, will become hungry ghosts. Tormented by a bloated and achingly empty belly, and a throat painfully constricted to block the passage of any substance, it is the fate of the hungry ghosts to roam the world causing pain and distress to ordinary law-abiding citizens. Should they attempt to eat, the food will burst into flames and burn their throats. For the Chinese, no worse fate can be imagined.

Some stories have suggested that a large number of bones were discovered as the town was being extended around the turn of the century. A discovery of bones might indicate, to the unromantic scholar, the un-

沒有男丁，才招致不幸呢？他們又是否要孩子得到同情呢？這些象徵，背後隱藏的意義，都須要一一弄清。

"包山節"其實是打醮的一種，在其他地方亦普遍，却在長洲舉行得特別頻密和大型。長洲打醮每年都有舉行，其他地方則可能十年才舉行一次。打醮的意思是驅除污穢，而中國人通常認爲災難是由孤魂野鬼帶來的。那麼，這是否表示長洲就特別多災多難呢？爲甚麼？

答案可能在長洲的墓地找到，那裏，葬了很多死得不明不白的人（中國的習俗，某些富有人家很多時都會出錢替無主孤魂或戰時無故死去的孤魂安排殮葬）。正因爲死不瞑目，這些孤魂會變成"餓鬼"。據說他們的食道會收縮，不能進食，於是終日要空着肚子，四處飄泊，以致令奉公守法的居民生活困苦。而且，每當他們吃東西，食物就會變成火焰，燃燒他們的喉頭，這對於中國人來說，無疑是很不幸的。

還有一些傳說：本世紀初，正當市鎮開始發展時，發現了很多人骨。這些人骨的發現，對於一些學者來說，代表五千年以來，居住在長洲的居民，一旦死去，並沒有像現在一樣得到安葬。可是，甚至有人誇大說長洲發現了大墓穴，死者都是那些被海盜所殺，而又得不到家人安葬的人。但這個說法似乎有很多疑點。首先，若果長洲曾經是海盜的避難所，海盜肯定會找別的地方埋葬受害者，好使亡魂不會麻煩他們。再者，如果死者被埋葬得那麼近原居地，那麼一些居民必定會世代相傳這段歷史。所以，這個說法雖然很動聽惑人，卻沒有足夠資料支持。

"包山節"的源起可追溯到一八九四年，那年長洲發生了一次嚴重的瘟疫，造成了無數死亡。而對上一個世紀前，亦有相類似的慘劇發生，那時居民仰神庇佑，北帝果然大顯神靈，驅走瘟疫。結果，居民更集資興建北帝廟，以謝神恩。可是，一八九四年的一次瘟疫，北帝却未能顯靈。

於是，一位島上的潮州人突然自稱北帝附體，若能到各家各戶舉行法事，即可驅走瘟疫。最初，沒有人理會他。但是，他依然強調擁有北帝法力。於是，居民決定給他一試。結果，他往幾戶作法，但似乎並不成功。再過了幾天，他繼續表現古怪的言行，最後更宣佈需要一張以劍做成的椅子，並特別指明尖的那端向上。居民果然替他弄來一張椅子。他坐在自己的"皇座"

marked graves of residents who have died in the previous 5000 years that the island has been inhabited. The idea of confining graves to cemeteries is, after all, of very recent origin. However, a more fanciful interpretation has expanded this story into the discovery of a mass grave containing the remains of unfortunate hostages, captured by pirates, whose families would not ransom them. The story, though, falls down on many counts. If Cheung Chau was once the haven for pirates, they would certainly have made sure their victims were killed elsewhere, if only so that the ghosts would not trouble them. Again, if they were buried so close to the original community there would have remained some knowledge of these mass-acres in the communal memory. Whilst an engaging and colourful story, it seems to have no basis in fact.

Cheung Chau's Bun Festival dates from the year 1894, when there was a serious outbreak of plague, resulting in a large number of deaths. A century earlier there had been a similar epidemic which Pak Tai is credited with curing, ridding the island of pestilence. It was due to this miracle that the present Pak Tai temple was built. In 1894, however, Pak Tai seemed unable to help.

Instead, the story goes, a man, a native of Chiu Chow, suddenly announced that he was possessed with the spirit of Pak Tai. He claimed he could save the island from the plague if he were carried in state from house to house. At first no-one paid any attention to him. However, he continued to act in a state of possession so it was decided to give him a trial. He was taken to a few houses, but without success. For a few more days he continued to act strangely, finally announc-ing that a special chair had to be constructed of knives with their sharp blades facing up-wards. This was done and seated on this new 'throne', with his arms and feet resting on yet more blades, he was again carried from house to house around the island. At the end, not only did he get off completely unharmed but, incredibly, it is said the plague left the island almost immediately.

From this beginning has developed the gaily coloured procession of floats we know today. But this is only one aspect of a very complete festival that now unites all the vying political factions on the island.

Nowadays, the first act in the proceedings is the selection of the time for the festival itself; it can take place on any three days in the first 15 of the fourth month. The selection is made by Pak Tai himself. On a certain day in the third week of the (Chinese) New Year, the chairman of the organising committee prays to Pak Tai to nominate the first day and then, naming each day in turn, he asks the god to give approval. He does this using two crescent-shaped pieces of wood called *sing pui*. Each piece has a flat side and a rounded side. The question is asked and the *sing pui* thrown on the ground. A 'yes' answer is obtained if they land with one flat and one rounded side facing up. The same method is used to select the chairman of the *Ta Chiu* commitee, a process which can last several hours. All the nominees and officiating priests come from the Hoklo or Chiu Chow communities, as only they have control of the Pak Tai cult.

In the week before the festival, the papier-maché gods are constructed at the site, the largest being more than 15 feet high. All are made in the same way, with the head, arms, legs and torso being constructed separately from strips of rattan tied around a bamboo shell. On this, paper is plastered and then painted to create the highly decorated bodies. The last act is the moment of fitting the head, thus bringing the god to life. In the temple forecourt, one can also see the buns being strung together.

中，被抬往各家各戶。結果，他不單完全沒有半點傷痕，而最奇怪是蔓延全洲的瘟疫果然立即消失。

所以，長洲現時的飄色，大概應是從那時開始發展出來。但是，飄色只是眾多團結島上不同政治派系的項目之一。

發展至現在，第一個程序是先在玄天上帝殿前"杯卜"擇日，擇定"打醮"應在農曆四月哪天舉行。具體情況是：每年正月十六日，先由上屆總理主持擇日，通常他會向北帝禱告，逐日提名該月的頭十五日，直至玄天上帝同意為止。用來卜問的是兩個半月形的聖杯，杯型是一邊平一邊圓，主持者先提出日期，然後把聖杯拋出，如果聖杯平的一面向着地，圓的一面向天的話，即是說北帝選擇那一天。除了醮期以外，該屆建醮值理會的總理亦是這樣卜選出來的。而透過這方式卜選出來的總理和大法師都必定是鶴佬或潮洲人，儼然是他們主宰了崇拜北帝的習俗。

建醮之前一個星期，在北帝廟前的康樂廣場，工人已開始用混凝紙製造各種神像，其中最巨大的甚至有十五呎高，而頭、手、腿和身軀分別用藤條紮在不同竹殼上，然後再用塗上了

灰泥和顏色的紙密封。身體各部份裝飾好後，
最後一個步驟是把頭裝上，這樣，神像便算大功
告成。此外，廣場另一角落，很多島上居民都
積極幫忙，女人串包，男人搭架。至於麵包師傅，
則大多忙於製包，更於包上印上 "福"、"祿"、
"壽" 等吉祥字眼。

　　曾經贊助 "包山節" 的團體或人士，均可
獲贈燈籠，高掛於門外。燈籠愈大，代表捐款
愈多。建醮前夕，大法師更會宣讀所有捐款人的
名字，然後，名單將會附在一頭紙白馬身上
一併焚燒。大法師隨即以香燭將四周街道淨化。
此後三日，便正式進入 "包山節" 的高潮。期間，
則須齋戒沐浴，禁絕殺生（可是，蠔和淡菜等
貝殼類食物則例外）。至於建醮值理會的總理，
則須齋戒整整一個月。

　　建醮的第一天，諸神被迎請到北帝的神壇，
醒獅、麒麟齊集等候點睛，居民亦到來禱告，
香火十分鼎盛。中午時分，大法師為神功戲主持
開壇儀式，手搖大扇、唸唸有詞，在五張放滿食物
的桌前作福。第二天則較為慼靜，居民可安享
各種視聽娛樂。最多姿多彩的會景神鑾遊行，

For this whole week, much of the town is engaged in the various preparations. The women string the buns, the men build the towers. Every baker on the island is involved in making the buns, each of which is stamped with a character wishing "good fortune", "good health", or "long life".

Lanterns are distributed to all those who have subscribed to the expenses, these being hung up at the house entrances along the alley-ways. The size of the lantern indicates the size of the donation. On the evening before the festival starts, the names of all the donors are read out by the priests. The list is then placed in a white paper horse and ceremonially burnt. The priests then race round the streets sweeping them clean with incense. Now, and for the next three days, the festival is in full swing. Meat-eating is forbidden; vegetarianism is the order of the day (though oysters, mussels and other shell-fish are allowed as 'honorary' vegetables). The chairman of the committee is supposed to have been vegetarian for the whole of the previous month.

On the first day of the festival the other gods are brought to pay homage to Pak Tai and stay with him in his altar. The lions come to be blessed; people come and pray; the air is thick with incense smoke. At midday, the priests conduct an opening ceremony on the stage of the opera house, running around five tables set out with food while chanting and waving large fans. The second day is quieter, a time for taking pleasure in the sights and sounds. It is on the third day that the main procession takes place. This is led by a golden statue of Pak Tai, followed by the other gods in their altars. Behind them comes Pak Tai again, but this time in his most venerated form as the black statue. The floats follow last of all.

In the old days, the gods would be taken in slow and solemn procession along the waterfront to the Kwan Yin Temple at the far end of the town. There, they would turn and race as fast as they could to get back to the Pak Tai Temple; great luck would befall the winners. By all accounts this was a rough affair in which men could be seriously injured or even killed. One year, the team carrying the god Hung Hsing grabbed the statue out of his palanquin and raced to victory carrying him in their arms.

Nowadays, all that remains of this race is a short jog for the last 50 feet. All along the route of the procession the streets are crowded and the balconies thronged with spectators. A second procession takes place on the day after the festival, when all the other gods are escorted back to their shrines. After the first procession, on the final evening of the festival proper, the focus in the temple courtyard turns to the bun towers. Now it is time to feast the hungry ghosts. A man is sent to the cemetery with a lighted lantern, it being his job to call out to the ghosts their invitation to the feast. As he will have to stay there until about midnight, this is not a job that is highly sought after. One informant claims that nowadays the only volunteers are desperate drug addicts!

Behind the bun towers, an area has been set up as a banqueting hall for the ghosts. There are 36 'tables', each set out with a cone of buns, food offerings, lanterns and incense sticks. Guarding the entrance way to this stand the three papier-mâché deities. In the centre is the benevolent, pale-faced figure of To Tei, god of the earth. On his left is a red-faced, grimacing god with a number of flags protruding from his back. These mark him out as the military general Shan Shen, the god of hills and mountains. Finally, on To Tei's right, is an even fiercer brown-faced giant, his foot raised menacingly in the air.

This is Dai Sze Wong, the lord of the underworld who torments the spirits of the sinful dead. Between the horns on his head,

則安排在第三天舉行。節日開始，金色北帝像率先出現，諸神隨後，跟着才是最受尊崇的黑色北帝像。至於其他飄色隊伍，則會接着登場。

從前，諸神行列會沿着海傍，向着位於市鎮盡頭的觀音廟，莊嚴緩慢地進發。到了那裏，飄色隊伍會鬥快折回北帝廟，因為他們相信，誰最快，誰就會得到好運。可是，這類型的比試往往會造成嚴重的傷亡。有一年，某隊伍因求勝心切，更將＂洪聖帝＂移離聖椅，抱在懷中，拼命跑回北帝廟。

現時，則只有到最後的五十呎，才舉行象徵式的短程慢跑。儘管如此，沿途仍有無數居民及旅客在大街小巷、露台窗戶吶喊助威。而第二次會景巡遊之送神歸廟，則在醮期完結後第二天舉行。

第一次會景巡遊結束後，就是大規模水陸超幽宴。這時候，最吃力的就是找一位提燈籠的人，到墓地等候至午夜，負責知會＂餓鬼＂。據一位居民透露，現在只有癮君子才願意做此苦差。

大包山後面，是專為＂餓鬼＂而設的超幽宴大廳。那裏有三十六張＂桌子＂，每張桌上放着一座小包山、祭祀用的食物、燈籠和香燭等。負責看守入口的，是三個紙糊的神像：居中是灰面慈祥的土地公；左面是紅面威武的山神；至於右面則是棕面兇猛的大士王。

大士王乃主宰地獄孤魂的神靈，祂的兩角之間，則有一個觀音像，用來提醒他要善待腳下孤魂。事實上，觀音亦負責管束大士王。一些迷信的說法更認為小孩在祂腳下行過，就可得到好運。在大士王身旁的則是 "地獄判官"，專責紀錄及核批生死。居民固然希望他寬大為懷，所以也稱他做 "仁慈" 判官。至於其他體積較小的灰色神像，則是大士王的部屬。最後，當夜幕低垂，這批神像就會一一取下焚燒。而大士王則排在最後。

大士王負責看守那些暫時被大法師釋放出來的 "餓鬼"，而大法師則通過神鏡，觀察 "餓鬼" 用膳情況，一待看見最後一隻 "餓鬼" 用膳完畢，即會發出訊號，結束幽宴。但，問題卻是這隻 "餓鬼" 難得釋放出來，肆食無厭，不肯罷休。於是，大法師使用竹條藐打大士王，然後焚燒，以期趕 "餓鬼" 回地獄。而在尚未禁燒炮仗時，所用的方法則是直接將大士王炸毀。

最後，幽包可以從包山取下來，分派給島上居民。而一般人相信，如果手上的幽包是從越高處取下來的，享有的榮譽也就越高。現時，取

however, is an image of Kwan Yin, goddess of mercy, whose presence is a reminder to him to spare the souls of these unfortunates who, one imagines, he is trampling under his feet. It is her job also to control him. Superstition holds that young children should walk under his boot for good luck. Interestingly, on Cheung Chau, Dai Sze Wong is more commonly known as Dai Shu Wong, Shu meaning tree in apparent reference to earlier forms of worship. Possibly, it was thought a tree's roots reached down into the underworld.

Next to Dai Sze Wong stands a small dark-cloaked figure, the so-called 'lenient magistrate' of the underworld who keeps a record of the living and the dead, and judges accordingly. One certainly hopes that he is lenient! The other small grey figures are the minions of Dai Sze Wong. As evening falls, all the figures are taken down and burnt.

Dai Sze Wong, the most important of the three, is last. He stands guard over the banquet tables while the hungry ghosts, temporarily freed from their constraints by the chanting of the priests, gorge themselves. The senior priest can now be seen looking through a monacle at the banquet. With the aid of this eye-glass he is able to see when the last hungry ghost has had his fill. At last, he gives a signal to show that the feasting has ended. Now the problem is that the last hungry ghost, having been given plenty to eat, is unwilling to remove himself and must be encouraged. This is achieved by beating the image of Dai Sze Wong with bamboo sticks and, finally, burning it. In the days when fireworks were not illegal, he was literally blown to smithereens by a giant firecracker.

Now the buns may be taken down from the towers and distributed to the people of the island. It is thought the buns nearer the top have greater honour. Nowadays, the buns are taken down by a few selected individuals; the square is deserted. This wasn't always so. In the past, late in the evening, the square would have been packed solid for the culminating moment, the scramble for the buns. At a signal, all the young men in the crowd would rush to be first to the top, thereby earning great merit and distinction. In 1976, a rather intoxicated European resident caused immense outrage by joining in and reaching the top of one of the towers first. There was talk for a few months of throwing the European residents off the island. Fortunately, tempers eventually cooled.

At this time, each of the towers was sponsored by organisations reputed to have close links with certain triad organisations connected to the Chiu Chow and Hoklo communities. As a result, the race to the top was a symbolic battle between rival triads, and the level of aggression was high. Not surprisingly, there was a very large police presence. Visitors to the island were closely vetted and anyone recognised as a triad member was immediately put on the first ferry back to Hong Kong. This triad involvement was an embarrassment to the authorities who were concerned to reduce the festival's status. Their opportunity came in 1978. As the scramble was getting underway, the middle tower suddenly yawed violently as the main bamboo support snapped. It swung to the side, hitting the right-hand tower before collapsing over the railings along the sea wall. Up to 30 people were seriously injured, and since then the scramble has been banned. As a result, the climax to the festival has gone.

Psychologically, this has had an emasculating effect. Now the festival ends with a fizzle, not a bang. There is no catharsis. Each year since, there has been a loss of

幽包的工作是由幾個特別挑選出來的人負責，所以廣場顯得十分清靜。然而，以前的情況是：一到黃昏，廣場上便擠滿等候搶包山的人，當聽到訊號，便即湧上包山，希望鰲頭獨佔。一九七六年，一個醉酒的外籍居民竟然爬上了包山頂，取得最高的一個幽包，結果導致居民不滿，甚至嚷着要把外國人趕出長洲，對抗氣氛持續了好幾個月。幸而，糾紛最後終於平息。

那時，包山都是由與潮洲及鶴佬社羣有聯系的三合會組織贊助建成，所以，能否搶得放在最高處的一個包，便成為不同三合會組織的一場意氣之爭，以致大批警察，亦須在旁維持秩序，而任何遊人若被發現與三合會有關，便會即時用渡輪送回香港。三合會參與包山節活動，實在令有關當局十分尷尬。結果，一九七八年，機會來了，當搶包山進行得如火如荼的時候，中間一座被搶得當場倒塌，並盪向右邊的一座，引致超過三十人嚴重受傷。自此，搶包山遂被正式禁止，而包山節的高潮亦宣告一去不復還。

搶包山被禁，頓然使這個節日失去了陽剛氣，並結束得了無聲色，遑論什麼高潮。自那年開始，節日的氣氛更一年比一年差。以前，飄色隊伍往往多過二十隊，現在，有十隊參加已算萬幸；以前，齋戒期內，偷食肉類，會被唾罵，甚至責打，現在，飄色一過，燒豬便隨處可見；
以前，邀請贊助，完全不成問題，現在，却要政府
贊助建做其中兩座包山，而第三座則在艱苦
籌集的情況下方能建成。現在，更謠傳政府受到
其他離島反對，是否繼續贊助也成疑問，而
島上居民亦以沒有時間爲"理由"，不想參與其
事。包山節的前景實在未許樂觀。

impetus: each year there is a diminuition of
ritual. Where once there were more than 20
floats, now they are lucky if they can get
10. Where once anyone caught eating meat
before the priests ceremonially dedicated a
pig after the midnight bun climb was loudly
rebuked and even beaten, now roast pork is
brazenly displayed after the procession has
passed. Before there was no problem getting
sponsors, now the government sponsors two
of the towers and the organising committee
has difficulty raising the money for the third.
There are rumours that the government subsidy is opposed by representatives from
neighbouring islands so even the government subsidy may be in doubt. Many people
now excuse themselves from involvement
saying that they don't have time. Sadly, the
future of the festival does not look rosy.

In writing this essay, I have been greatly helped
with information from Lyn Austin, Pat Lam, Man
Kwok Chung, Robert and Kan O'Brien and Julia
Wilkinson. Thanks also to Bernadette, my wife,
for all her translating work.

Jonathan Chamberlain is the author of *Chinese
Gods*.

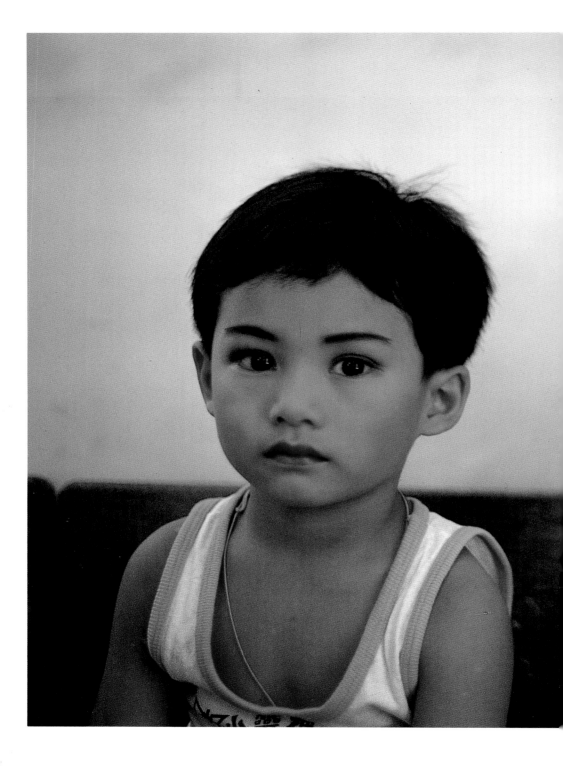

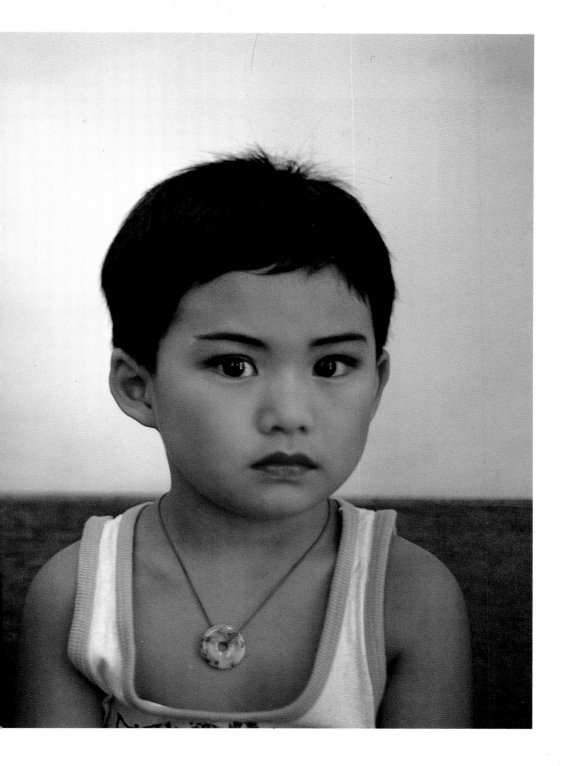